Our
Hysterical
Heritage

Inquiries should be directed to
Stemmer House Publishers, Inc.
2627 Caves Road
Owings Mills, Maryland 21117

Published simultaneously in Canada by
Houghton Mifflin Canada Ltd., Markham, Ontario

A Barbara Holdridge book

Printed and bound in the United States of America

First Edition

Library of Congress Cataloging in Publication Data

Main entry under title:

Our hysterical heritage.

    1. Children—Anecdotes and sayings.   2. Presidents—United States—
Election—Anecdotes, facetiae, satire, etc.   I. Dunn, Harold.
PN6328.C509   818'.5'402   79–22777
ISBN 0–916144–50–X
ISBN 0–916144–51–8 pbk.

Harold Dunn

Our Hysterical Heritage

The American Presidential Election Process, Out of the Mouths of Babes

illustrated by Victor Curran

1980

Stemmer House

PUBLISHERS, INC.
Owings Mills,
Maryland

Introduction

When you're teaching school during a presidential election year and a student tells you that "politicians are getting closer apart in their thinking," you know it's going to be a year filled with whimsical observations.

Whimsical, charming, beguiling, unwittingly penetrating—all accurate descriptions of youngsters' comments about presidential elections. I've always thought that children's humor is the funniest kind of all because it's so honestly spontaneous and truly human.

Many years ago, when I first began publishing their captivating comments—wishing to share the moments that can be so full of surprises and glimpses into what is really going on in a child's mind—I wrote under a pseudonym, believing that a few parents might think I was holding their children up to ridicule. Since then, I have found that without exception, they realize that we grownups can only envy the beauty and poetic simplicity of a child's manner of expression.

As you read along you may be struck, as I was, by the way children have of seeing into the real meaning and value of the election process in a democracy— and doing so with a wisdom supposedly beyond their years. Even as you smile, you glimpse a truth hidden underneath. Childish observations like these say with laughter what many a teacher has tried to say, but less successfully.

Kids are fresh, original and offbeat in their communication because that's the only way they *can* be. They're not like us adults who can reach into our lifetime stockpile of common expressions for a ready-made way of saying what we wish. The child has no stockpile, and so he's forced to think through his ideas for himself and then *make up* an expression that seems to fit. You will find, in fact, that most youngsters seem to lose any and all inhibitions when they express their opinions about presidential elections.

I've always admired the men and women who make the personal sacrifices required of anyone who stands for office. We can't all do it, but we *can* be as knowledgable as possible about candidates and issues and long-range policies. A lesson our nation learned early and well is that each citizen had better take an active interest in running his country or he may suddenly find the country running him.

Grade-school youngsters haven't reached that point yet. They're still grappling with the fundamentals of the presidential election process—and not always winning. As in everything else, there is such a profusion of facts to be absorbed that some get lost or mishandled in the rush. Their comments may be foggy, but sometimes—in a roundabout way—they hit a great truth right on the nose.

And their insights may well go with us right into the polling booth.

Harold Dunn

Ballwin, Missouri
January 1980

Contents

Our
Hysterical
Heritage

George Washington said no president should be sentenced to more than two terms in the Big House.

Looking at history as children sometimes see it is like looking through the wrong end of a telescope. Trying to remember names of historical personalities is a puzzler even for grownups, but few people have ever been quite as confused as the boy who confided: "Daniel Webster once thought he would like to run for president. He should not be confused with Noah Webster, a king from the Bible who reigned for 40 days and 40 nights."

Now let's follow a trail of very small footprints into America's past and see what else the youngsters have to say about democracy at work in American history:

For quite some time there was Earth but no America. This greatly slowed up the progress of elections.

The people in Egyptian times invented 365 days in a year, but true democrasies improved it by sticking in an extra day every four years for elections.

The Medieval Ages failed to develop their government. They only got as far as kings and could not think how to have any monarchy like we do.

The idea of electing a president every four years was founded by our forefathers. They founded it where it had been put. It had been put in the Constitution all the time.

Our nation was still in its infanthood when our foundling fathers thought oughtn't we to hold elections?

One of the first laws passed by Congress was the Law of the Land. It said no fair having America without having a President.

Thomas Jefferson believed in everybody's right to have four fathers.

I do not remember for sure when James Madison was born but I understand he is older than he looks.

George Washington said no president should be sentenced to more than two terms in the Big House.

While Madison was president in 1812, the White House had a fire and burned down everything that happened in the way.

President Monroe was a tall slender-haired man.

Where did Abraham Lincoln receive his greatest acclaim?
In history.

Peter Cooper was the presidential nominee of the Greenback Party in 1876. The Greenback Party was in favor of making all money legally tender.

After his term as president was over, Teddy Roosevelt went on an expedition to shoot big game including his wife.

Grover Cleveland figured out how to be both our 22ond. and our 24ourth. president. He did this by getting beat by our 23ird. president.

Friendshipwise, Theodore Roosevelt and William Taft were at first veryclose.

James Buchanan was elected president even though
he was accused of being a batchelor.

Theodore Roosevelt and William Taft were at first friends but later became contemporaries.

Both sides of Woodrow Wilson were well educated.

All in a sudden the tensity of the situation was changed. Wilson was elected.

When the final votes were in it was found that Wilson was only slightly elected.

When they told Charles Hughes he was not president after all he was very ambarist.

So he only missed by a whiskey being elected.

The 19th. Amendment said women could vote. This brought about universal suffering.

When Hoover was running for re-election in 1932, the depression was like an Albert Cross around his neck.

Lincoln's life teaches us the advantage of enjoying what we have, even if there isn't any.

Name three Democratic candidates since 1944.
Lyndon Johnson is one and I bet you can guess the others.

Franklin Roosevelt was the longest president of the United States.

When Roosevelt triumphed, he triumphed hard.

The chief value of the election of 1944 was to help remember the date of.

Despite what the polls said were going to happen, Harry Truman defeated Thomas Dewey in 1948. Many believe over-confidents was Dewey's chillies heel.

President Truman's re-election in 1948 is sometimes called a political miracle because it was something that could not happen until after it did.

Was President Truman's 1948 campaign a front porch campaign or a whistle stop campaign?
Yes.

William Bryan was nominated for president in three different Democratic Convents.

Then Eisenhower and Nixon appeared on the rostrum and acknowledged the thunderclap of noise.

Eisenhower and Stevenson were the first candidates to do much flying in the campaigns. All those before them had stuck pretty close to terra cotta.

Adlai Stevenson cut short his visit in London and took the first planet home.

Compare the election of 1960 with that of 1964. 1964 was found to be more modern.

In 1964 everybody was just taking it easy and then it all got four years later and here came another election for president.

In 1968 the weather was pretty nice throughout the country and voters took advantage of it as over 70 million of them went to the pools.

A total of 39 presidents are all part of our hysterical heritage.

If all the Republicans who met in San Francisco for the 1964 Convention were to stand single file around the convention building, it would surprise many people.

Thinking about
who to be it
is one of our constant doings

One trait of the very young is that they don't let facts get in the way of their imagination. Every classroom is a gathering of little poets, philosophers, doers and dreamers. Some youngsters have imaginations that soar away at the slightest touch, like kites on a summer day. If you're at all hazy about the selection of candidates, hang on. Here are some "imaginary facts" that will prove more thought-provoking than reality.

The Democrats and Republicans are the mainest parties in the United States. Minority parties are called third parties. There are about 30 third parties in all.

It is important to have good men elected to president. Without good presidents we would maybe be starving, freezing and having nothing to wear.

Thanks to democracy, we now know when a person votes he is somebody and not just a person because democracy shows us that everybody equals everybody else if they are Americans.

Once I was elected president. I was elected president of my third grade class last year only I did not know what to do about it.

Some of the values of cilivization are it teaches people to have conventions and campaigns and fight to be president in a cilivized way.

When my fellow-sister said she did not like the Democrats I had hateful feelings of anger and flew into a tirage.

The more I think about trying to run for president the less I think of it.

Citizens of the United States may be either Republican or Democrat and male or female upon reaching the age of voting, if of good moral character.

I have found candidates to be extra talkity people.

The difference between a king and a president is that a king is the son of his father but a president is not.

The president has the power to appoint and disappoint the members of his cabinet.

We have a White House. We have a president for it. Thinking about who to be it is one of our constant doings.

The most important duty of 1976 was to get a president decided.

How many people will vote in the next election is not a very interesting number.

What I learned about elections is that we aren't really getting to elect the president. It is some people in a college who get to. I have not decided what to do about it yet but I am not going to just sit around.

Much has been said about balancing the budget. It has been found that budgets are more talkable than balanceable.

Sometimes I cannot help wondering where our leaders are coming from. No president has been born for over fifty years.

As I watched the convention on television, it was rather pleasant to hear their voices and realize that they were 1000 miles away.

Sometimes state party committees change hands. Except they are not the flesh and boney kind of hands. Just the party worker kind.

If you want to know a year ahead of time who is going to be a party's presidential candidate, you can always write and ask the National Committee Chairman to get no hint at all.

If his father is a politician, the son is likely to get into politics while he is still green behind the ears.

Once upon a time Daddy started to listen to a convention on television. "Just then mother said no you must help me." Daddy saddened noticeably but that was the end of that happening.

We need elections more than just once every four years. Think about it. See!

Splinter groups are things that get in bandwagons.

George Bush is my favorite candidate because I don't really know much on him.

I was experienced by speaking to Mr. Baker over the week end who once shook hands with President Truman. Mr. Baker eats oats for breakfast and re-members when the first atom bomb exploded. Think of it.

Yesterday I thought how it would be best for Carter or Reagan or Connally or any of them to try hardest for those states with the most electoral votes. Except it had already been thought of.

I once heard about a Ronald Reagan who was governor of California, but I don't know whether it was he or him or who.

The chances of Jimmy Carter winning all the electoral votes in 1980 are smaller than a naked eye.

It is o.k. with me for Howard Baker to get to be president because I already know how to spell Howard Baker.

Being nominated
means watch out unless you
don't mind being elected

Children are always observing, thinking and trying to put it all together. Much of the fun in talking with kids comes from the startling way they can put a backspin on their answers, saying something that's absurd and sensible at the same time:

The teensiest part a convention can be divided into is a delegate.

Being nominated means watch out unless you don't mind getting elected.

Candidates have kept politicians from going crazy. For if they held a convention and did not have any candidates, they would be crazy.

Convention halls are so wonderfully built that more people get in them than is possible.

All I know for sure about unit rule is that I don't know for sure what it is.

What are the three steps we learned are necessary to nominate a presidential candidate?
The first step. The second step. The third step.

I plan to report on alternates because of the important sound of their names.

Grassroots in politics are unusually different from in real life.

What follows the nomination of the presidential candidate on Wednesday?
Thursday.

Some people believe that national nominating conventions might well be abolished after 1980. What is the soundest reason for this viewpoint?
The sound of everybody at the conventions yelling all the time.

Every seat in the galleries were filled. Hundreds
of persons were turned down for seats.

After the chairman uses his gavel to tell each dem-
onstration he wants silence, they go on silently toot-
ing their horns and such for a while longer.

If I was at a convention, I would make a stiffly-worded speech about how the candidates should think more about we lay-children even though we cannot vote for them.

These smoke filled rooms are where they go and after a lot of fighting and lickering they finally agree on a candidate.

Until it is decided whether a favorite son is a candidate or not, everyone has to keep calling him a favorite son.

A caucus is something people vote in. Sort of a small booth.

The job of delegates is to resent their states.

Ever so often party state chairmen resign. This is when their seats are vaccinated.

If some law said the Republicans and Democrats had to meet at the same convention, people might have to stand closer together but their ideas would probably be even farther apart.

One of the strictiest rules is all dark horses running
for president must be people.

A gift is not always needed for a present. A delegate can just sit there and still be present.

Candidates usually like to wait for awhile before they tell everybody they are a presidential aspirate.

What does the phrase "Splinter Group" mean?
It means ouch.

During these demonstrations, a sea of humanity floods the isles.

When a reporter there says the convention hall is quiet, then it is not noisy. But if he says it is quite, you must keep listening. He has not finished telling you.

An overwhelming favorite is a candidate that often comes over to the convention and whelms the delegates. He is so far ahead he can do whatever he wants to.

Calling a person a runner-up is the polite way of saying you lost.

An alternate would be called a co-delegate if it did not look so funny.

Nomination convictions are where everyone expresses their convictions about who should be nominated.

Sometimes these conventions look like big parties. But they are not called parties because that word has already been taken by the Democratic and Republican parties.

An election is when it is between Democrats and Republicans. But in nominating conventions Democrats get to fight Democrats and Republicans fight Republicans.

Even if you get nominated by your party you still don't get to be president yet, so oh well.

Then at the end of the balloting when they all know who the candidate will be, they shout their vote for him anonymously.

Anxious to start his worldwind campaign, he left the convention floor, got into his limasine and started off in all directions.

The difference between a caucus and a cactus is how you pronounce it.

The nominees are usually called candidates or campaigners, although I have heard them called other things.

I think a unit rule means the same as a bloc vote, but now I forget which both means.

A grassroots campaign is only an imaginary expression but people still get elected by it.

Sometimes a candidate worries that even if he is nominated he will not be able to get enough money to be elected. But that is a worry in the future tense. Most candidates know not to cross their chickens before they are hatched.

Nominate is to do for party what vote is to do for country.

At times landslides get started at these conventions. But somehow they manage to go on with their convention.

Nomination conventions are louder than the largest known sound.

For campains,
take two aspirants
every four years

Obviously, a child's mind is a vast storehouse of miscellaneous misinformation—half true, half false and wholly delightful. One of the fringe benefits of teaching is the possibility that the next paper I read will contain a "wrong" answer that is twice as captivating or thought-provoking as the expected one:

Every four years America is struck by presidential campains.

One of the mainest rules of campaigning is you are not allowed to go on a whistle stop tour without a train.

What campaign managers manage is to explain things.

When they talk about the most promising presidential candidate, they mean the one who can think of the most things to promise.

Without votes, candidates could win very few elections.

One of the main by-products of presidential campaigns is interrupted programs.

What is a national ticket?
What policemen give you if you don't be a good citizen and vote.

A candidate has to stand and talk and think. Campaigning is hardest on the ends of him.

Elephants and donkeys never fought until politics came along.

The words "Take the stump" started in early days when a candidate would use a tree stump as a speaker's platform. I have heard at least one person who claimed this was interesting.

Did you ever think what I used to think about candidates running neck and neck? Well it is not true.

Politician is the bawling out name for a candidate you don't like.

Some campaign speeches are so hard to understand, it is often impossible to know what has been said without listening to them.

Speeches are easier to listen to when the speaker makes sure he prounces the words right.

Everybody wanting to be on the side of the winner is a condition known as bandwagon.

Thin skinned is good in apples but bad in candidates.

Most presidential campaign tours are enough to make the average person drop from pure exhausteration.

Trying to be everywhere at once keeps them going like a horse afire.

Campaigns consist mostly of candidates.

When a presidential candidate visits a city, the police usually stretch an accordian along his motorcade.

Political strategy is when you don't let people know you have run out of ideas and keep shouting anyway.

When they asked how many of us had or had not listened to the political discussion last night, it was found that very few of us had or had not listened.

Issues are when they tell what they advocake and what they don't.

Candidates need to show carefulness in their statements and their promises and their et ceteras.

So much speech making often causes their throwts to get orangitis.

A canvass can help find out how people are thinking. As far as I know, that is its only talent.

The main job of a candidate is to get everybody to vote. But a good citizen is a person who does not have to be reminded to vote, so he does it without listening to any candidate.

As soon as he finished speaking, Secret Service men whiskied the candidate off to a waiting car.

A candidate should always renounce his words carefully.

Acknowledging the introduction, he turned to undress the audience.

The campaign speech began promptly fifteen minutes late.

A poll is sometimes taken to tell a candidate how bad beat he is.

We are learning how to make our election results known quicker and quicker. It is our campaigns we are having trouble getting any shorter.

I have not yet had many enjoyments from hearing campaigns.

The hardest part about being a candidate is getting elected.

What poll takers have found out about always predicting who will be president is they can't.

Being that time of year, the candidates have to
watch out for bad coeds.

Speaking of defeat, candidates are told never to.

Campaigns give us a great deal of happiness by their finally ending.

Whoever wins gets to be president for four years because that's how long it is before we can stand to have another campaign.

During the 1980 campaign, income taxes will be a rich source of arguments.

What will indicate if interest in the 1980 presidential election starts falling?
That the law of gravity is still with us.

The 1980 election is really more important than its name sounds.

Whatever else he does, a president isn't a very good president unless he sees to it that peace rages near and far.

All about election and inoculation day

Oliver Wendell Holmes once observed: "Pretty much all the honest truth-telling there is in the world is done by children." Through the years, most of my students' comments about elections and inaugurations have proved to be unexpected, unconventional—and true:

One of the main qualifications is to get more votes than anybody else.

A president must be an inhabitant of the country in which he lives.

It is possible to get the majority of electoral votes without getting the majority of popular votes. Anybody who can ever understand how this works gets to be president.

The campaign is when the candidate tells what he stands for and the election is when the voters tell if they can stand for him being elected.

Actually, elections are different from politics. Elections come and go while politics are with us all the time.

The 1976 campaign had everything a good campaign should have such as candidates.

We are only supposed to vote on presidents every four years. Stop the election until we see if 1980 can divide itself into four.

One of the unusualities about our elections is that there has only been two candidates on each party's ticket up to the time of so far.

Elections are one of our country's most essential pasttimes.

One of the oldest of all American election customs is to come in November.

X's are practically extincted today except for voting and kissing.

There is no use trying to elect a president without electing a vice president. It's just one of those things.

Some other countries have very, very democratic elections. But the elections in America are very, very, very democratic.

Elections are good for democracy and having tests about.

Elections are not held every November. They are held every four Novembers. You see once they get started, elections last at least four times as long as the average November.

Elections are made for exciting waitings.

Elections use two types of machines. Voting and big city.

We have our election the first Tuesday following the first Monday during November. Now it might seem strange why we hold it in this type of language. Well the reason is if the first Tuesday came after a Wednesday say, then we know something is wrong so everybody stop voting.

People get to vote but computers get to say who will be president.

We select our president the first Tuesday after the first Monday in November. We call it Selection Day.

Holding an election is not like holding something in your hand. You have to go to a booth.

America has been electing presidents by the voting method for as long as I can think to remember.

In America today, a president and vice president from different parties is an unrule.

It may work for other choosings, but eeny meeny miny moe is not a good way for president choosings.

When you are voting for president no you are not. Your voting for someone to go to an election college. Just because, I guess.

In the voting booth people vote by ballot or machine. In the electoral college it is said that they vote by custom.

Even after a person is elected, he must consintrait and remember to be there on his swearing in day.

Before taking office, the president must raise his
right hand and take some oats.

Electric computers are the first to know who is going to be president. Then they tell who can go to an electric college and make it official.

If the number of votes received by two candidates are identical, they equal each other as long as they are the same.

Many of our presidents have been people who were born right here in America.

A victory celebration is a custom left over from the times when people were happy.

Another thing Inauguration Day means to me is Ber it's cold outside.

I put on my thinker as to when Inauguration Day is held. I thought hard, hard as a rock. Finely I thought out that I do not know.

An election won't take unless the winner is inaugurated.

The winning candidate is elected and inoculated.

It takes many months to get elected but it only takes a little nick of time to get inaugurated.

As the television camera looked down on the Inauguration Ball, I could see a mass of faces on the floor dancing arm in arm.

In January, the president makes his Inaugural Address after he has been sworn at.

What is the President's Inaugural Address?
Somewhere on Pencilvania Avenue.

The person who is elected president of the United States also gets to be president of the Executive Branch.

Once he is elected, sometimes the president has to work 24 hours a day until he finds out what he is supposed to do.

The people who are expected to help the president sometimes are locked up in his cabinet.

Dear President:
Boy are you in trouble

Once he is inaugurated, letters to the president start arriving from America's classrooms as thick as chalk dust. Some have the urgency of a telegram: "Send me both sides of the question immediately!" *Some are zany:* "abcdefghijklmnopqrstuvwxyz. how is that for handwriting?" *All are uninhibited:* "Stop reading your icky letters and get to work."

But the classrooms are not the only source of kids' letters to the president. One horrified parent found a cryptic note stuffed in a back corner of his ten-year-old son's desk drawer:

Dear President: Boy are you in trouble. Don't say I didn't warn you and it won't help you just to say oopps. Clomp Stomp Clomp. Listen. That is Dad coming to write you. Now I think I will say good by. Good by."

Here's one that ends with the finality of a dropped egg: "Dear president, I am not speaking to you."

You can't argue with this young writer. When she's through, she stops writing—which is a good example for grownups to follow.

We came across a problem in our arithmetic about our national debt. Do you know how big it is? In dollars and cents it is more than about 700 billion, that's all! Do you know how big that is? It is g-r-r-e-e-a-a-t BIG! Even over 10 times bigger than that. And do you know how many years it will take to pay it out at a million dollars a year? That happens to be the problem asked in the book. If you can tell me the answer I promose not to complain no matter how adsurb the answer is (in years remember).

Send me Lindas fingerprints. I'm pretty sure it was her.

Is this your right address? I have an important question I need to find out, but first I need your address. Is this it? If not don't worry allthough it was pretty important.

I paid Timmy the .27¢ I owed him so don't forget to minus it from the national debt.

Do you have a campain manager for our school yet? I would make a fine one. All of the 22 eligabally voting teachers here like me and I would use all my influenze on them. My fee would be unreasonably modest. What about it?

I am a future inventor. Tell me some of the inventions our country needs in the future so I can start on them now.

I didn't get your cherry blossom from Washington if you would like to send me one.

Oughtn't you to know that Jan keeps her fingers crossed when she sings the Star Spangled Banner?

Does the governmnt. give ayn free lessosns intyping?

Now that school is out, I am out of worries. For my patriotic duty I am ready to help you with one of yours. You may send two if you like during June.

I listen on the news to what you say each day. Where can I get a more simplefied way of hearing what you say?

I am a song writer and I already have five songs under my belt. Now I am going to tackle one about you if you will help me. Try to think of some of your good things about you. Ahhh don't be so modest. Tell them to me and I will work them in the song somehow.

It would mean a lot to me if you would do something. Please sing Happy Birthday in a letter to me.

How much does the government charge for parakeet autopsies? Hurry since he died day before yesterday.

Just for fun I had my historical ancestors traced and I think I am Royalty. Congratulate me! Thank you very much and who else should I let know?

I have decided you should be re-elected president in 1980. Please write and tell me why.

I have to draw a tree-diagram of our government and I am stuck on the Executive Branch. You are equal to the Senate and the House. Right? But does that mean one of you equals both of them or does just one of them equal you? Also if you know anything about the Judicial Branch tell me how many limbs I should make for that one too.

When you have a spare time I would like you to write me so I can show some of the nurds around here that I am on writing terms with President Carter. Some of the things you might mention are about how you hope I will be for you in 1980 and my amazing abilities at shortstop and with shadows. I think they will be able to know what you mean.

This is to show you how good I can write. If you cannot read it come and visit me and I will say it to you.

Definitions: Also-ran means goof in the language of politics

Youngters often misinterpret just a word or two, but that's all it takes to cause a comical kind of chaos. Psychologists tell us that half-learning a word incorrectly is often the first step to learning it right. As you study these definitions of some of our best-known political terms, I guarantee you'll find out things you never knew before:

The law of **adequate returns** says there had better be as many votes counted as there were people voting.

Also-ran means goof in the language of politics.

Alternate delegate is a more dingnified way to say substitute.

An **anecdote** is a kind of medicine candidates are always giving.

There is no such thing as an election **ballyhoo** but it makes a lot of noise when there is.

Blocs are easier to pronounce than to tell what they mean.

A political **canvass** is something spread out over grassroots to keep them from front-running.

Constituents are what people are except they can be chickens or practically anything you can get to vote for you.

The best thing about **conventions** is they are filled with adventurous excitement even though they are sometimes too noisome.

Corruption is when the party in power is making too much profit. If it is a smaller amount it is known as politics.

Constituents are what people are except they can be chickens or practically anything you can get to vote for you.

A **darkhorse** is a candidate that the delegates don't know enough about to dislike yet.

A **draft** is when somebody says he doesn't want to be president for so long that they make him be it to shut him up.

Election fever usually starts with the swelling of a convention hall and pretty soon spreads all over America.

Sometimes a state delegation nominates a nominee from their own state. They call him a **favorite son**. What the other nominees call him is unbeknownst.

A **floor fight** is when they call each other names in public as well as in private.

A **front runner** is the vice versa of a dark horse.

Grassroots are not what they sound like they are. I am not sure what they are, but they are not that.

A front runner is the
vice versa of a dark horse.

Heredity is a bad thing in politics because it gets us kings instead of presidents.

A **hullabaloo** is a small ballyhoo.

An **improvised speech** means to put on like they are just now thinking of it.

The meaning of **inauguration** is only for the president to have whispered in his ear.

An **Independent** is a Republican or a Democrat that cannot make up his mind which.

Political **instinct** is what tells a candidate the right thing to do and say. Extinct is when he is wrong.

When the radio mentions a **landslide**, cross your fingers and hope it is talking about an election.

A **minor party** is one that people under 21 are allowed to join.

When the radio mentions a
landslide, better cross your
fingers and hope it is
talking about an election.

75

Noncommittal is to be able to talk and talk without saying anything.

An **overwhelming choice** is like a frontrunner except even more that way.

Politeness is to say something good about your opponent while courteousness is not to say something bad.

Political science is to try to figure out what makes candidates act that way.

Politicians work at running. Oh. Not their legs just their parties.

Poll takers are not allowed to take the polls that people go to to vote.

A **poll tax** is a tax people pay for the enjoyment of going around asking people questions.

Popular votes tell who is the most popular. Electoral votes tell who is the most elected.

Noncommittal is being able
to talk and talk without
saying anything.

Presidential clemency is to make sure no man is hung twice for the same offense.

Primary elections are like primary grades. You should pass them before you try to be in public office.

A **quandary** is a thing a worried candidate gets into which is one good reason for all the worrying.

A **runner-up** is one who indulges in too much defeat.

Shoo-in is a campaign technique perfected by Franklin Roosevelt.

Political **slogans** are brief unnecessary sayings.

Smoke-filled rooms mean they are trying to figure out who to fire from running for president. It is just another case of where there is smoke there is fire.

Splinters are in groups when they are not in fingers.

Primary elections are like primary grades. You should pass them before you try to be in public office.

A **split ticket** is when you don't like any of them on the ticket so you tear it up.

A **squeak-in** is about 50 votes more than a neck-and-neck.

Political **ties** are just to get elected and not to wear.

Unit rule means everybody vote for one candidate in unanimosity.

Universal suffrage means that even the illegible get to vote.

Vice is something bad like a vice president.

A **whistle stop tour** is a tour of where they make all the whistles they blow at conventions.

A split ticket is when you
don't like any of them on
the ticket so you tear it up.

**Blank pages
for the reader's own
favorite "youngsterisms"**

Our Hysterical Heritage

Designed by Victor A. Curran

Text Composed by Typesetters, Inc., Baltimore, Maryland, in Melior and Quorum Bold

Printed and bound in paper and Kivar 9 Tangerine Llama by Fairfield Graphics, Fairfield, Pennsylvania, on 60 lb. Spring Forge Offset, vellum finish